W9-AYW-355

First Edition, June 1990.

ISBN 978-0-87083-526-1

Published by

Living Stream Ministry
2431 W. La Palma Ave., Anaheim, CA 92801 U.S.A.
P. O. Box 2121, Anaheim, CA 92814 U.S.A.

Printed in the United States of America

10 11 12 13 14 15 / 10 9 8 7 6 5 4

Salvation in Life in the Book of Romans

Witness Lee

Living Stream Ministry
Anaheim, CA • www.lsm.org

CONTENTS

PREFACE

This book contains translated messages released originally in Chinese in Taipei, Taiwan on April 25-27, 1990 by
Brother Witness Lee during times of fellowship with the
full-timers involved in the gospelization of Taiwan. These
messages have not been reviewed by the speaker.

CHAPTER ONE

REDEMPTION IN CHRIST'S DEATH AND SAVING IN HIS LIFE

Scripture Reading: Rom. 1:1-4, 17; 3:22-24; 5:10

I. The subject of Romans—the gospel of God—Rom. 1:1-4:
   A. Promised by God in the holy Scriptures—v. 2.
   B. Concerning the Son of God, Jesus Christ our Lord—v. 3a:
      1. According to the flesh—humanity, coming out of the seed of David—v. 3b.
      2. According to the Spirit of holiness—divinity, designated the Son of God in power out of the resurrection of the dead—v. 4.
   C. Explaining clearly that the just shall have life and live by faith—Rom. 1:17:
      1. The just—the one whom God justifies, to whom God has given His righteousness—Rom. 3:22-24.
      2. Out of faith—taking faith as the principle; righteousness being God's righteousness, which is out of God; faith being our faith, which is of us.
      3. Shall have life and live—receiving the eternal life of God and living by this life of God.
II. Christ's death and His life—Rom. 5:10:
   A. We being reconciled to God through the death of Christ—including being redeemed and justified—Rom. 3:24.
   B. We being saved in the life of Christ—the complete and full saving of God in Christ.
   C. These two becoming the gospel of God—the complete and full salvation of God.

Tonight, I will do a new thing which I have never done before. I will cover three messages in one evening. Furthermore, I will cover ten messages in three evenings. The main subject of these ten messages is salvation in life from the book of Romans. My purpose in giving these ten messages is twofold: First, I desire that you would receive help. Then, as you return to the gospel outreach localities, you can help the new ones message after message with the help you have received.

These messages contain an unprecedented understanding concerning the book of Romans which has never been found in Christianity. Though the way this understanding is presented is particular, it is not peculiar. These messages contain new light that we have received from the Lord. Because others have not seen these things before, they are new. They are rare and wonderful because no one has ever seen them. Hence, these ten messages are all new, fresh, and wonderful.

THE TWO GREAT SECTIONS OF THE BOOK OF ROMANS

I treasure very much the outline and sectional divisions of the book of Romans in the New Testament Recovery Version. I feel that they have been done in an excellent and concise way. However, tonight I will not speak according to them. Rather, I will give you something new. I will show you that Romans is divided into two main sections. Just as a watershed is a mountain with two slopes dividing a river into two sections, in the same way, Romans is divided into two sections by a watershed. This watershed is Romans 5:10, which says, "For if, while we were enemies, we were reconciled to God through the death of His Son, much more, having been reconciled, we shall be saved in His life." This verse is too precious! We had passively become enemies of God, and we also were behaving as enemies of God. At that time, we did nothing good. All that we did was to act as enemies of God. Even the sisters who look so gentle today were enemies of God before they were saved. But praise God, while we were yet enemies, God has reconciled us to Himself through the death of Christ His Son. This is one slope of the watershed. Having been reconciled, we shall be saved in His life. This is the other slope of the watershed.

One slope is the death of Christ. The other slope is the life of Christ. His death is for redeeming us, and His life is for saving us. These two terms are very different. Redemption plus saving is salvation. If we only enjoy redemption without being saved, we only have the first half of salvation. The biblical principle is always that that which comes first is not so good, and that which comes afterwards is better. For example, in John 2 with the sign of changing water into wine, the first wine was not the best wine (v. 10). The wine which came later was the best wine. In Numbers 18:17, the firstborn were to be killed, but those born afterwards were saved. To be redeemed is only the first half of God's salvation. This aspect of salvation is not that high. When one enjoys the saving in life—the second half of God's salvation, the experience of salvation is much higher.

Before Romans 5:10, there is the slope of Christ's death. From 5:10 until the end of the book in chapter sixteen, there is the slope of Christ's life. When you go back to your localities, you can tell others that Romans is divided into two sections. The first section is on Christ's death, and the second section is on Christ's life. Christ's death redeems us, justifies us, and reconciles us to God. This is full redemption. At the same time, the life of Christ saves us. The content of this saving is very rich. It is not as simple as redemption.

Being saved in the life of Christ can be divided into nine great items. None of these has been covered by others before. For example, the first item is that the law of the Spirit of life has freed us from the law of sin and of death (Rom. 8:2). The first item in the saving of Christ in life is a law freeing us. This law is the law of the Spirit of life. This law of life is the Triune God. The Spirit of life is the ultimate consummation of the Triune God. Hence, this God is the Spirit of life, and this Spirit of life is a law.

We know that a law comes from life. Life itself is a law. Every living creature is a law. The cat is a law. The dog is a law. The cow, the bird, and the fish are all laws. A human being is also a law. Hence, the cat lives a cat's life, the dog lives a dog's life, man lives a man's life, and God lives God's life. God is the highest living being. Hence, He is the highest law. Thank the Lord, this highest life is in us today. This highest life has become the highest law in us. This is the first item of the salvation in life in the book of Romans.

THE SUBJECT OF ROMANS—THE GOSPEL OF GOD

Promised by God in the Holy Scriptures concerning the Son of God, Jesus Christ Our Lord

According to the Flesh—Humanity, Coming Out of the Seed of David, and according to the Spirit of Holiness—Divinity, Designated the Son of God in Power Out of the Resurrection of the Dead

Our Lord Jesus Christ came out of David, the descendant of man, according to the flesh, according to His humanity. He was also designated the Son of God in power out of the resurrection of the dead, according to the Spirit of holiness, according to His divinity. Apparently, the word *designation* does not imply birth. Actually, designation means begetting. When Jesus died, He lay in the grave and was ranked with the dead ones. But in less than three days, He was resurrected from the dead. This resurrection marked Him out in a particular way. His resurrection from the dead designated Him the Son of God in His humanity. Hence, He was begotten the Son of God in resurrection. This proves that the resurrection of Christ is a birth (Acts 13:33). Originally He was the only begotten Son of God. After He became flesh, and through resurrection, He was born the firstborn Son of God in His humanity. At the same time, we were also begotten as the many sons of God in resurrection.

Explaining Clearly That the Just Shall Have Life and Live by Faith

The Greek word rendered *live* in Romans 1:17 has a double meaning. It means to have life as well as to live.

This sentence originally came from Habakkuk 2:4. In the New Testament it is quoted three times. First, it is quoted in Romans. Then it is quoted in Galatians 3:11. Last, it is quoted in Hebrews 10:38. In Galatians the emphasis is on having life. In Hebrews the emphasis is on living. But in Romans the emphasis is on both meanings: to have life and live.

You have to circle these three terms: *the just, faith, life.* When you go back, you have to teach the new ones. Tell them that Romans talks about the just, faith, and life. If you only talk about the just and faith, you are only up to Romans 5:10. After 5:10 it talks about justification unto life (5:18). Faith gives us justification, and the result is that we enjoy the life of God. Formerly, we were dead. After we believed in the Lord, we were justified. Moreover, we have life and shall live. Hence, after Romans 5:10, we are told how one should live after he has life.

The Just—the One Whom God Justifies, to Whom God Has Given His Righteousness

We are not just; we are sinners. When we believed in the Lord Jesus, God gave the Lord Jesus to us as His righteousness. The word *gave* means *to reckon*. It is like the reckoning in accounting. For example, you may owe someone eighty billion dollars and be unable to repay him. So, God gives you eighty billion and reckons it to your account. In this way, you no longer have any debt. Rather, you are justified.

Out of Faith—Taking Faith as the Principle

God reckons His righteousness to man out of faith, taking faith as the principle. It is not by work. Righteousness here is God's righteousness; it comes from God. Faith here is our faith; it is of us.

Shall Have Life and Live— Receiving the Eternal Life of God, and Living by This Life of God

God has a righteousness for us. Whether we can have it depends on our faith. Hence, we have to believe and receive right away, so that we can have this righteousness. God has righteousness, and we have faith. When these two combine, we receive God's eternal life and are able to live by this life of God.

THE DEATH OF CHRIST AND HIS LIFE

Through the death of Christ, we are reconciled to God. This includes redemption and justification (Rom. 3:24). We are saved in the life of Christ. This is the full and rich saving of God in Christ. Redemption plus saving equals the gospel of God, His full and rich salvation.

When you go back to your localities, you have to teach the new believers. You cannot do it the way I am doing it— teaching three lessons in one evening. Perhaps, you can only teach half a lesson every evening. You should do it slowly. You have to believe that this will lay a foundation in them. This is not man's word or man's teaching. It is the holy Word of God. When you transfuse them this way, the Word will get into them.

CHAPTER TWO

THE LAW OF THE SPIRIT OF LIFE FREEING US FROM THE LAW OF SIN AND OF DEATH

Scripture Reading: Rom. 8:2-13

I. The law of the Spirit of life having freed us—v. 2a:
   A. Life—the eternal life of God.
   B. The Spirit—the resurrected Christ who was transfigured as the Spirit.
   C. Law—the natural capacity, which is the person of the pneumatic Christ Himself as the embodiment of the processed Triune God.
   D. Freeing us—causing us to be released from bondage and to have freedom.

II. The law of sin and of death—v. 2b:
   A. Sin—the sin in the sinful nature, which is the evil nature of Satan, causing us to have the ability to sin.
   B. Death—coming from sin, causing us to have no ability to do good.
   C. Law—the natural sinning capacity in the sinful nature, which is the person of Satan himself as evil itself.

III. The processed Triune God making the three parts of our being life:
   A. The Spirit of Christ being the pneumatic Christ entering into our spirit and making our spirit life—vv. 9-10.
   B. The Spirit and our spirit mingled as one spirit, spreading into our mind to make our mind life— v. 6b.

      C. The resurrecting and indwelling Spirit of God reaching our body, making our body life also—v. 11.

IV. The cooperation we should render:

      A. Setting our mind on the spirit—v. 6b.

      B. Walking according to the spirit only—v. 4b.

      C. Putting to death the practices of the body by the Spirit—v. 13.

NINE ITEMS OF SALVATION IN THE LIFE OF CHRIST

Let us first consider the nine items of salvation in the life of Christ. The first item is the law of the Spirit of life freeing us. The second item is the subjective and dispositional sanctification. The third item is the renewing of the mind, resulting in transformation. The fourth item is the building up in the Body of Christ. The fifth item is the conformation to the image of the Son of God. These are the five basic items. None of these five items are things we have ever thought of in our own mind. When you return to your localities, you have to teach the new ones properly, item by item.

After these five items of saving, there are four results: reigning in life, living in the church life, crushing Satan under our feet, which brings in God's kingdom, and our bodies being redeemed and glorified.

THE LAW OF THE SPIRIT OF LIFE FREEING US

Life denotes the eternal life of God. The Spirit denotes the resurrected Christ who has been transformed into the Spirit. The law is the natural capacity. Every matter has its nature, and within its nature is a power, a capacity. For example, steel and iron have the capacity to be very hard, resistant, and durable. They can also sever and cut things. These are their capacities. But wood has a different capacity.

The law of the Spirit of life within us also has its nature, its essence. It also has its natural capacity. This capacity is the person of the pneumatic Christ Himself. This law is personified; it is just Christ Himself. He is the embodiment of the processed Triune God. Hence, this law is just the Triune God. He is not just a thing, but a person who frees us. Sin is also a person. We can never overcome sin. But the law of the Spirit of life releases us and gives us freedom.

THE LAW OF SIN AND OF DEATH

The law of sin and of death is also personified. It denotes the sin in our sinful nature, not the sins in our conduct. The sin in our nature is the evil nature of Satan. It causes us to have the ability to sin. Death and sin may be considered as twins. Where sin is, death is always there. Sin causes man to have the ability to commit sin. Death comes from sin and disables man from doing good. These twins reside in man, causing him to be weak in performing good, but strong in committing sin. As a result, man is finished and cannot do anything anymore. This is the condition of man since the fall. Paul describes this pitiful condition of man in Romans 7. At the end of the description, he said that he was a wretched man (v. 24) without any strength to overcome the law of sin and of death.

THE PROCESSED TRIUNE GOD
MAKING THE THREE PARTS OF OUR BEING LIFE

How does the Triune God turn the three parts of our being into life? In Romans 8 we first see that the Spirit of Christ is the pneumatic Christ, who has entered into our spirit to make our spirit life (vv. 9-10). Our spirit has been made alive. Our spirit has not only been made alive, it has also become life. The Spirit has "life-ized" our spirit. Second, the Spirit is mingled with our spirit to become one spirit. This mingled spirit then spreads into our mind—the main part of our soul that surrounds our spirit—and makes our mind life. This means that when we set our mind on the spirit, our mind is life (v. 6b). Third, the resurrecting and indwelling Spirit of God reaches our body (v. 11), resulting in our body receiving the dispensing of life.

The way our whole person is turned into life is from the center to the circumference, from the spirit through the soul to our body. First, God makes our spirit alive. Then, He makes our soul alive. Finally, He makes our body alive. Ultimately, all three parts—our spirit, soul, and body—become life. At present, we can experience our spirit and soul coming alive. But our body has not been fully transformed. When our body is redeemed and in glory, it will also be fully alive. Thus, it will become life. Today, at times we are weak in our body and sick. By exercising our spirit, our body can be somewhat strengthened. This is a foretaste of our body becoming life.

THE COOPERATION WE SHOULD RENDER

First, we have to set our mind on the spirit (Rom. 8:6b). Second, we have to walk only according to the spirit (Rom. 8:4b). Third, we have to put to death the practices of the body by the Spirit (Rom. 8:13). Whatever the body desires to do, we would reject. We must wait on the order from the Spirit before we allow the body to act. Suppose you know that it is not good to go to the cinema and that it is good to go to the meeting hall for a meeting. You must remember that if you decide out of your own will to go to the meeting hall, it is still death. Your going to the meeting hall must be the result of the leading of the Spirit. This is why you have to put to death the practices of the body, whether they be good or bad. You have to tell the Lord, "Lord, I would not go to the cinema, nor would I go to the meeting hall. I would go wherever You want me to go." If the Lord wants you to go to the meeting hall, you may go there. But which meeting hall should you go to? Should it be Hall Three, or Hall Nine? If you choose by yourself, then it is your own move again. You must stop and allow the Spirit to give you the leading within. Perhaps the Lord would not want you to go to Hall Three or Hall Nine. Perhaps He would lead you to go to Hall Two. When you go this way, it will be the move of the Spirit.

We must not merely do good works; we must follow the leading of the Spirit. We must put to death the practices of the body by the Spirit. We must walk only according to the spirit. This is our necessary cooperation. I hope that when you go back to your localities, you can explain these riches to the new ones you are helping. If you do this, you will be a faithful minister of Christ, able to plant the living word into man.

CHAPTER THREE

THE SUBJECTIVE AND DISPOSITIONAL SANCTIFICATION SAVING US FROM A NATURE SOAKED WITH THE ELEMENT OF THE WORLD

Scripture Reading: Rom. 1:7a; 15:16b; 6:18, 22b, 19b

I. The two aspects of sanctification:
   A. Positional sanctification—Rom. 1:7a.
   B. Dispositional sanctification:
      1. Saving us from a nature soaked with the element of the world.
      2. In the Holy Spirit—15:16b.
      3. Our cooperation:
         a. Presenting ourselves as slaves to righteousness—6:18, 22b.
         b. Presenting our members as slaves to righteousness—6:19b.

II. The fruit of subjective and dispositional sanctification:
   A. Causing us to be sanctified dispositionally and occupied by God—6:19b.
   B. The end of our being sanctified dispositionally unto God being eternal life—6:22b.

When man fell, his whole person became the world. He was fully soaked with the element of the world. Therefore, God's sanctification comes in to deal with the world. Sanctification means separation from the world. Since God wants to sanctify us dispositionally, He must deal with the worldly element in our nature. There is no one who does not love the world. Even children are no exception. After man fell, his inward nature was soaked with the element of the world. Now, as soon as he sees anything of the world, he desires it. Hence, after we are saved, we need to have a subjective and dispositional sanctification that will separate us from our nature that is soaked with the element of the world. For man to give up his love for the world is not an outward act. It is a sanctification in man's inward nature. When his nature is inwardly sanctified, he spontaneously will not love the world. When you teach all these points to the new ones whom you serve, you must do so in a slow way, mouth to mouth, point by point, so that they all will be able to understand.

THE TWO ASPECTS OF SANCTIFICATION

Positional Sanctification

When we are first saved, we experience positional sanctification (Rom. 1:7a). Matthew 23:17 uses the gold of the temple as an illustration. The gold was originally common in its position. Some was sold at the shops, and some was stored at home. Some gold was beaten into rings and worn on the fingers. But when it was put into the offering box, the gold's position was transferred from a common place to a sanctified place. At that time, the gold was positionally sanctified.

Dispositional Sanctification

Since we, the sinners, have been soaked by the element of the world in our inward nature, we not only need an outward change in position, but we also need inward dispositional sanctification. First, this sanctification delivers us from the nature that is soaked by the element of the world. Second, it puts us in the Holy Spirit (Rom. 15:16b). When we are in the Holy Spirit, we will not argue with others easily. On the contrary, we will be fully at peace with others.

We cooperate by presenting ourselves as slaves to righteousness (6:18, 22b) and by presenting our members, one by one, as slaves to righteousness (6:19b). For example, we may have used our mouth to argue with others in the past. But when we present our mouth to righteousness, we present it for speaking thanksgiving and praise. Thus, it is no longer used to argue with others. The use of our ears is another example. Our ears may have loved to listen to gossip about the shortcomings of others. But now when we are about to listen to these things, we can declare to Satan, "Get behind me. My ears have been presented as slaves to righteousness. I will no longer listen to these words. My ears are for listening to the word of God." This is dispositional sanctification.

THE FRUIT OF SUBJECTIVE
AND DISPOSITIONAL SANCTIFICATION

When we cooperate with the Lord to present our members as slaves to righteousness, the fruit of this sanctification causes us to be separated dispositionally and to be occupied by God. Our lips are occupied by God, and our ears are occupied by God. The more we are occupied by God, the more God's life increases in us, and the more we enjoy God Himself. Hence, the end of our being sanctified dispositionally unto God is eternal life (6:22b).

AN ADDITIONAL WORD

The outlines that I am giving you are clear and concise. They give you a good example. When you go to the villages to teach the new ones, you have to teach them point by point. You must not teach in a wrong way. If you teach wrongly, it will be difficult to change the new ones. I hope that we would all carefully keep this point. When we teach the truth, we must speak accurately.

Moreover, when we speak, we have to learn to speak

slowly, with proper variation of tone and with proper rhythm. We have to learn this. For those of us who are working for the Lord, most of our work involves speaking to others. The key to speaking is not whether we think that we have spoken clearly or not, but whether others have understood our speaking or not. If others do not understand us, then our speaking will have no result. Hence, we who are working for the Lord have to learn to speak. What we speak must be something that others can understand and comprehend.

CHAPTER FOUR

THE RENEWING OF THE MIND
AND THE RESULTING TRANSFORMATION
SAVING US FROM A LIVING SOAKED
WITH THE ELEMENT OF THE WORLD

Scripture Reading: Rom. 8:5b, 6b; 12:2, 5-11

I. The renewing of the mind:
   A. The result of setting the mind on the spirit—Rom. 8:6b.
   B. Minding the things of the Spirit according to the spirit—Rom. 8:5b.
II. The resulting transformation:
   A. The transforming of the entire soul, with the mind being its principal part—Rom. 12:2.
   B. The result of not conforming to this age being saved from a living soaked with the element of the world—Rom. 12:2a.
   C. That we may prove by testing the good, well-pleasing, and perfect will of God—Rom. 12:2b:
      1. Being members one of another with the saints, coordinating to be the Body of Christ, and living the Body life in it—Rom. 12:5.
      2. Also coordinating and serving with the saints in the Body of Christ for the building up of the Body of Christ in order to accomplish God's New Testament economy—Rom. 12:6-11.

The life of God in Christ saves us in five aspects, and brings in four results. The first result is that we reign in life to subdue all kinds of insubordination. Thus, we take control of all kinds of environments. Second, we are enabled to live the church life in a locality, being saved from our self-view and self-goal. Every one of us has his own view. It is the church life that saves us from our own view. If a church is full of opinions, it is no longer normal. It becomes Laodicea. Man's views and opinions produce different goals. These different goals hinder the church from being built up. The third result is the crushing of Satan under our feet which brings in God's kingdom. Last, the ultimate consummation of God's salvation in life brings us into glorification.

Tonight I want to tell you again that in order to be in the Lord's work, you must first have the vision. The vision governs the view. Our view has to be governed by the vision. Second, we must not form parties. To form parties has to do with our private interests and personal goals. The phrase to *form parties* has been translated in the Recovery Version as *factious, strife,* and *rivalry* (Rom. 2:8; 2 Cor. 12:20; Gal. 5:20; Phil. 1:17; 2:3; James 3:14, 16). People are in strife and rivalry because they have their own personal goals and are for their private interests. The result is problems.

LEARNING THE SECRET THROUGH
THE DIFFICULTIES IN THE LORD'S RECOVERY

Six months ago, a brother insisted on seeing me and tried to fellowship with me concerning the present problem in the Lord's recovery. I told that brother that I have been in the church life for fifty-eight years and have become very familiar with these kinds of things. They are like the cycles of metabolism of the body; after a while the body gets sick for a time.

During the eighteen years that I was in mainland China, Brother Nee was responsible for the ministry of the word. During those eighteen years, I saw at least four storms. In 1949 we moved to Taiwan and began the work here. During this period of forty years, the cycle of storms has been a little farther apart. But the storms have still occurred about once every ten years. The seed of the first problem was sown as early as 1957. By 1959, the seed had almost sprouted. This incident had much to do with my burden to go to the West.

In 1962 I was clear that the Lord wanted me to pick up the burden to begin His recovery work in the United States. I remained there until 1965 before coming back to Taiwan to clear up the situation. At that time the church was pursuing the life messages on the Gospel of John. In chapter two the Lord told the Jews, "Destroy this temple, and in three days I will raise it up" (v. 19). At that time I told the brothers and sisters that if the work in Taiwan was of the Lord, even if man were able to destroy it, the Lord would raise it up again in resurrection.

We have to see that there is no sea that does not have storms, and there is no human being who is never sick. Some sicknesses make men weak. Other kinds of sicknesses can eventually make a person strong. All parents know that children have to go through sicknesses before they can grow up well. If a child is rarely sick, he could die of a sickness when he does become sick. This is because he does not have a defense system built up within him against sickness. For this reason, though it is not a good thing to be sick, we do not have to be afraid of it. Today I am eighty-six years old, and I have passed through many serious sicknesses. First, I had tuberculosis, then I had a stomach disorder, and eventually I had an ulcer. After passing through a few serious illnesses, I have become even stronger than before. Hence, do not be afraid of difficulties. Difficulties are very beneficial to the organic growth of the church.

THREE FACTORS IN THE WORK OF THE LORD

During the past few decades, the problem among us has been that some have the ambition, but they do not have the capacity. If a man does not have the capacity to reach the goal of his ambition, he will be like a disgraced politician. Whether in the church or the work, the problem lies in this point. In addition to capacity, there must also be the proper heart. We should be pure in our heart and single for the Lord's recovery. Only then will we be a help to the recovery. This is like a person engaged in world government. If he has the ambition and the ability to do something for his nation and his people, and if his motive is pure, he can become a hero to the nation and a savior to his people. But if he has the ambition and the ability, yet lacks a pure motive, he will become a problem. The same principle can be seen in the Lord's recovery.

In 2 Corinthians 5:9 Paul said, "We are ambitious...to be well-pleasing to Him." At that time, Paul was also very capable. He not only received gifts from the Lord, he was also very well-educated in Greek and Hebrew. He was taught at the feet of Gamaliel (Acts 22:3) in the city of Tarsus, a city which had the highest academic institution of the time. He had a strong academic foundation. Fourteen Epistles in the New Testament were written by Paul. His Greek was fluent, and his logic was sound. Peter and Mark's writings could not match his. In their writings we cannot find terms such as *economy, mystery, the eternal purpose of God,* etc. John was a Galilean fisherman. His style was to express the mysterious things with simple words. For example, he said such things as: "I in them, and You in Me" (John 17:23); "In the beginning was the Word, and the Word was with God, and the Word was God" (1:1); and "In Him was life, and the life was the light of men" (1:4). All these are simple words, but these words contain mysteries within them. This is the characteristic of the books of John.

Paul, however, wrote in Romans, "But I see a different law in my members, warring against the law of my mind..." (7:23). In chapter eight he said, "For the law of the Spirit of life in Christ Jesus has freed me from the law of sin and of death" (v. 2). Because Paul wrote of such deep things in his Epistles, we sometimes wonder whether or not the believers who received his letters were able to understand them. Today we are able to understand what a law is because modern science has advanced so much. In Paul's writings, there are indeed many mysterious things.

I encourage you young ones to have ambition. But we still have to look to the Lord to give us the capacity as well

as a pure motive. Only when we have all three can we
become useful in the hands of the Lord. Otherwise, sooner or
later, we will become a problem. May the Lord be merciful
to us.

THE RENEWING OF THE MIND
AND THE RESULTING TRANSFORMATION

The mind is the principal part of the soul. In some places
in the New Testament, the mind and the soul mean the
same thing. Our mind is renewed within by the renewing
Spirit. This is only the beginning. The renewing Spirit
spreads from our mind to our whole soul, which is composed
of our mind, will, and emotion. The mind, will, and emotion
together with the conscience in the spirit compose our heart.
The renewing of the mind is the renewing of the whole soul of
man together with his spirit. Hence, transformation results
from the renewing of the mind. Romans 12:2 tells us that we
are "transformed by the renewing of the mind." First, our
spirit is regenerated. After our spirit is occupied by the Lord,
the Lord Spirit then spreads from our spirit to our mind.
When our mind is renewed, we are brought on until our whole
soul is transformed.

Transformation is not the same as change. It is the result
of a metabolic process. I have used this example many times.
Tonight I will use it again. When a person's complexion is
not good, he can put on powder and cosmetics to improve
his complexion. But this is not transformation; it is only a
change. What then is transformation? Suppose your face is
yellow and pale and looks appalling. If you will eat nutri-
tious food in the right proportions, the food in your body
will produce a metabolic change in you after it is digested.
On the one hand, this metabolism provides you with fresh
supply. On the other hand, it eliminates the old elements.
Gradually, your pale and colorless complexion will be gone,
and your face will shine with a rosy complexion. This is not
a change; it is transformation. The Lord Jesus is our life.
When he enters into us, he becomes a supply to us. This
supply produces an effect in us. It eliminates the old and

the natural elements from us. In the end, we are transformed and are full of His image (2 Cor. 3:18).

SAVED FROM A LIVING SOAKED
WITH THE ELEMENT OF THE WORLD

After we are transformed by the renewing of the mind, a power will be produced in us that saves us from a living soaked with the element of the world. Romans 12:2 says, "And do not be conformed to this age." To be conformed to this age is to be modern. This verse says that we should not be conformed to the modern way of this age. To be modern is to be fashionable; it is the appearance of this world before our eyes. I have experienced the simplest rural life, and I have also lived in the most modern cities. I discovered one thing: everyone likes to be modern. Whether the modern way is good or not, man loves it just the same. Everything that is modern and that is in conformity to this age is welcomed by man. But we have to know that the age of this world and the modern way of this world are common and unsanctified. Hence, we must not be conformed to this age. Rather, we should be renewed in our mind and be transformed in our soul. This will save us from a living soaked with the element of the world.

Setting the Mind on the Spirit
and Minding the Things of the Spirit
according to the Spirit

To be renewed in our mind, we need to set our mind on the spirit daily. The result will be the renewing of the mind. While we are in the church life today, no matter what happens, and what needs there are, we have to set our mind on the spirit. We should not set our mind on what is right or wrong, or on our views. We must set our mind on the spirit. This will result in our mind being renewed.

Renewing is different from brainwashing. Renewing is the total replacement of all of man's thoughts, notions, and conceptions. Brainwashing, on the other hand, is like putting powder on a person's face. Renewing is an inward metabolism. When the Lord's life and His Spirit enter into man, there is a turn. Furthermore, to be renewed in our mind is to hand over to the Lord our concepts, perceptions, and views through loving Him and fellowshipping with Him, and through saying to Him, "Lord, I take You as my life, my view, and my way." He is constantly operating within us. In this way, our whole mind is renewed, and within us we will have a different view toward the world than we had before. This is not a change. This is an inward transformation in life. Hence, we have to set our mind on the spirit (Rom. 8:6b). This will bring in the renewing of the mind.

Furthermore, we have to mind the things of the Spirit according to the spirit (8:5b). We should not mind the things of the earth and should not be conformed to the age.

That We May Prove by Testing
the Good, Well-pleasing, and Perfect Will of God

Now we are qualified to understand the will of God (12:2b). According to Romans 12, the will of God is for the saints mutually to be members one of another, coordinating to be the Body of Christ and living the Body life in it (v. 5). Furthermore, we coordinate and serve together with the saints in the Body of Christ for the building up of the Body of Christ in order to accomplish God's New Testament economy (vv. 6-11).

CHAPTER FIVE

BEING BUILT UP TOGETHER IN THE BODY OF CHRIST TO BE DELIVERED FROM THE INDIVIDUALISM OF THE NATURAL LIFE

Scripture Reading: Rom. 12:5, 1, 2, 8b-21

I. The purpose of God's New Testament economy:
   A. To make sinners the members of Christ to be constituted the Body of Christ—Rom. 12:5.
   B. To be the fullness—the corporate expression—of the processed Triune God.

II. All the saints being built up together in Christ to be one Body:
   A. Presenting our bodies a living sacrifice to God— Rom. 12:1.
   B. Being renewed in the mind for the transformation of the soul—Rom. 12:2.
   C. Burning in spirit and serving the Lord always— Rom. 12:11.
   D. Living an excelling life by the divine love, a life as high as caring for enemies—Rom. 12:8b-21.

III. Enjoying the salvation in life to be delivered from the individualism of the natural life:
   A. Not being isolated and peculiar.
   B. Caring for others and forgetting oneself.

After renewing, we come to know the Body. Now we will consider how to be built up together in the Body of Christ to be saved from the individualism of the natural life. If we are unwilling to live the Body life, we are individualistic. Man is prone to be individualistic. Even when he is young, he finds it hard to get along with his parents and his brothers and sisters. He also cannot readily coordinate with others. This proves that the natural life of man is individualistic. However, God's salvation in life is to deliver us from this individualism so that we can be built up together in the Body of Christ.

THE PURPOSE OF GOD'S NEW TESTAMENT ECONOMY

The purpose of God's New Testament economy is first to make sinners the members of Christ so that they can be constituted the Body of Christ (Rom. 12:5). The third stanza of *Hymns,* #541 speaks of this truth:

> Not philosophy nor
> Any element
> Can to Christ conform us
> As His complement;
> But 'tis Christ Himself who
> All our nature takes
> And in resurrection
> Us His members makes.

This is a miniature of Romans 12. This hymn was written thirty years ago and shows that the light was very clear among us concerning this matter even in 1960. We can see that to constitute sinners as the Body of Christ is fully a matter of life. The purpose of God's New Testament economy is to make this Body the fullness, the corporate expression, of the processed Triune God.

ALL THE SAINTS BEING BUILT UP TOGETHER
IN CHRIST TO BE ONE BODY

First, we have to present our bodies a living sacrifice to God (Rom. 12:1). Second, we have to be renewed in the mind for the transformation of the soul (v. 2). Third, we have to be burning in spirit to serve the Lord always (v. 11). Fourth, we have to live an excelling life by the divine love, a life which is so high that it would even care for our enemies (vv. 8b-21). This kind of life is not found in the world. It far excels all philosophies throughout the ages. The Confucian ethical teaching in China is quite profound. But it never goes as deep as to teach one to love his enemies, or to feed them when they are hungry, or to give them water when they are thirsty, or to supply whatever they lack (12:20). This life reaches such a height that it even loves its enemies. Today, in the church life, we should excel to such an extent that we love our enemies. If we can love our enemies, we can surely love every member. But if we cannot love our enemies, then it will be difficult to love the members, and the Body life will not be realized.

ENJOYING THE SALVATION IN LIFE
TO BE SAVED FROM THE INDIVIDUALISM
OF THE NATURAL LIFE

Salvation is redemption plus saving. Redemption is brought to us by the death of Christ, and saving is brought to us by the life of Christ. In the outline at the beginning of this chapter, we preceded the word *salvation* with the word *enjoying*. This means that the salvation in life is to be enjoyed. Its taste is sweet. Hence, you must not only understand these truths and the way to present them, you must also learn when and how these truths should be presented according to the circumstances so that your expression of these truths can be more attractive. After we enjoy salvation in life, we can no longer be isolated and peculiar. Instead we will care for others and forget ourselves. Thus, we will be saved from the individualism of the natural life.

CHAPTER SIX

BEING CONFORMED TO
THE IMAGE OF THE SON OF GOD
TO BE DELIVERED
FROM THE EXPRESSION
OF THE NATURAL LIFE

Scripture Reading: Rom. 5:10; 8:29-30; 1:17b; 6:19b, 22b; 12:2; 8:19

I. God's original creation of man:
   A. That man may have His image to express His glory and beauty.
   B. That man may receive Him as life to live by Him.
II. The result of man's fall:
   A. Destroying the image that God created for man.
   B. Losing the position of receiving God as life.
III. Christ's redemption by His vicarious death and His salvation in life—Rom. 5:10:
   A. Redeeming fallen men so that they may be justified by God and reconciled to God—Rom. 8:30.
   B. Then regenerating, sanctifying, renewing, transforming, and conforming them to the image of the Son of God—Rom. 1:17b; 6:19b, 22b; 12:2; 8:29:
      1. Making them sons of God—Rom. 8:19.
      2. That Christ may become the Firstborn among many brothers—Rom. 8:29.
      3. That God may gain a corporate expression which is the mingling of His firstborn Son with His many sons.
IV. Enabling the believers to enjoy God's salvation in life and to be delivered from the expression of the natural life:
   A. Having no self-boasting.
   B. Having no self-esteem.

GOD'S ORIGINAL CREATION OF MAN

In Genesis 1, God created man with His image to express His glory and beauty. Then in chapter two, we have the tree of life, which signifies God's intention for man to receive Him as life and to live by Him.

THE RESULT OF MAN'S FALL

When man fell, he destroyed the image that God created for him, and lost the position of receiving God as life. The image that God created for man is one of love, light, holiness, and righteousness. These things are the very essence of the Ten Commandments in the law, and they were created for man by God according to His own image. God is a God of love. Hence, He created love for man. God is a God of light. Hence, He created light for man. God is a God of holiness. Hence, He created holiness in man. God is a God of righteousness. Hence, He created righteousness in man. But after man fell, he destroyed this image that God had created for him. In addition, God had barred the way to the tree of life by the cherubim and a flaming sword which turned every way to keep the way of the tree of life (Gen. 3:24). We were unable to be reconciled again to God and to enjoy salvation in life until Christ died for us and redeemed us.

CHRIST'S REDEMPTION BY HIS VICARIOUS DEATH AND HIS SALVATION IN LIFE

Christ's redemption by His vicarious death and His salvation in life first redeems fallen men so that they may be justified by God and reconciled to Him (Rom. 8:30). In addition to this, He regenerates, sanctifies, renews, transforms, and conforms them to the image of the Son of God (Rom. 1:17b; 6:19b, 22b; 12:2; 8:29). This conformation to the image of the Son of God begins from regeneration. After regeneration there is sanctification. After sanctification there is renewing, and the renewing brings in transformation. When all these items are added together you have conformation to the image of the Son of God. Furthermore, we will be made the sons of God (8:19) that Christ may become the Firstborn among many brothers (8:29). Thus, God gains a corporate expression, the mingling of His firstborn Son with His many sons. In this way, we are enabled to enjoy God's salvation in life and are delivered from the expression of the natural life, having no self-boasting or self-esteem, and are conformed to the image of the Son of God.

Part of the third stanza of *Hymns,* #52 says:

> He leads the praise! How precious to Thine ear
>   The song He sings!

This shows us that it is most pleasing to God for the firstborn Son to lead the many sons into the praise of God the Father. The second and third stanzas of *Hymns,* #1 say:

> As we view the vast creation,
>   Planned with wondrous skill,
> So our hearts would move to worship,
>   And be still.
> But, our God, how great Thy yearning
>   To have sons who love
> In the Son e'en now to praise Thee,
>   Love to prove!

Actually, the many sons are in the firstborn Son. In other words, the firstborn Son includes the many sons. It is a corporate Son that is praising and exulting God. This is a profound truth. But it has been written into a hymn and is explained in very simple words. I hope that you can all enter into these truths and can teach them to the new ones.

CHAPTER SEVEN

REIGNING IN LIFE TO SUBDUE ALL KINDS OF INSUBORDINATION

Scripture Reading: Rom. 5:16-17, 18b, 21; 8:2

I. God justifying the believers that they may have life—Rom. 5:18b:
   A. Justification dealing with sin for the believers—Rom. 5:16.
   B. Having life dealing with death for the believers—Rom. 5:17.
   C. The life received becoming the law of the Spirit of life that frees the believers from the law of sin and of death—Rom. 8:2.

II. God causing the believers to have life that they may reign in life—Rom. 5:17:
   A. Subduing the insubordination of sin, death, and all the negative things belonging to sin and death.
   B. Sin reigning unto death, and death reigning through the sinner, causing the sinner to lose all his rights—Rom. 5:21a, 17a.
   C. Grace reigning through righteousness unto eternal life, and eternal life through Jesus Christ causing the believers to reign—Rom. 5:21b, 17b:
      1. Bringing in God's kingship.
      2. Expanding to be the kingdom of God, which is the increase of Christ as the seed of God's kingdom.

In this and the following chapters, we will consider the results of God's salvation in life. The first five items speak of God's salvation in life. The first item is the law of the Spirit of life. This law saves and frees us. Second, we have the subjective and dispositional sanctification that saves us from a nature soaked with the element of the world. Third, the renewing of our mind leads to the transformation of our whole soul which delivers us from a living soaked with the element of the world. Whereas dispositional sanctification delivers us from a nature soaked with the element of the world, the renewing of our mind, leading to the transformation of our soul delivers us from a living soaked with the element of the world. Fourth, we are being built up together in the Body of Christ, and are thus delivered from the individualism of the natural life. Last, we are also being conformed to the image of the Son of God to be delivered from the expression of the natural life. These five items of saving in life are very profound. They touch the depths of our being. They touch our nature, our living that is soaked with the element of the world, our individualism in the natural life, and the expression of our natural life.

There are also four results to the saving of the life of Christ. First, we reign in life to subdue all insubordination. When we come to the matter of reigning, we reach the top and the ultimate point; there is nothing higher than this matter. God has saved us to the extent that we can reign in this saving life. The second result is that we are all living the church life in a locality to be saved from our self-view and self-goal. The third result is that Satan is crushed under our feet and God's kingdom is brought in. The final result is that we reach glorification, the ultimate consummation of God's salvation in life.

CHRIST BECOMING THE PROPITIATION SACRIFICE

All of you who are involved in the spread of the gospel work should know that after we bring a person to salvation, we must help him to know Christ's redemption through His death. The first step of redemption is to redeem us back. The second step is justification based upon this redemption.

Then we are reconciled to God. The meaning of reconciliation is to appease. In the New Testament Recovery Version, we used the term *propitiation* (1 John 4:10). Formerly, we sinned and developed a problem with God. We had violated His law. At the same time, through our sins, Satan took the opportunity to inject his poison—the sinful nature—into us. As a result, we were unable to live with God in peace.

God is willing to bless us. But on our side, we have developed a problem with Him. Therefore, there is the need of propitiation. Christ came to be our propitiation. He did not come to appease God's wrath, for God's wrath was not greater than His love. He still loves us. That is why He sent His Son to be our propitiation (1 John 4:10). Propitiation is not to appease God's wrath, nor to appease our problem. It is to appease the sins that we have committed before God. Christ has come to solve for us the problem of sin. The solution of the problem of sin is His appeasing.

REIGNING IN LIFE TO SUBDUE
ALL KINDS OF INSUBORDINATION

In the Old Testament, there was atonement, but not redemption. The day of atonement was on the tenth day of the seventh month each year (Lev. 23:27). The sacrifice offered was called the sin offering. In addition there were the trespass offering, the burnt offering, the meal offering, and the peace offering. The meal offering had neither blood nor flesh. Its contents were flour, oil, and frankincense. All the other four offerings, however, contained flesh and blood. The sin offering deals with the deep-seated sinful nature in us. The trespass offering deals with our outward, sinful conduct. When the Lord Jesus died on the cross, His death was a sin offering; it dealt with our sin. John 1:29 says, "Behold, the Lamb of God who takes away the sin of the world." The sin here refers to the totality of sin, including the inward sin and the outward sins—the nature of sin and the acts of sin. In Chinese theology, there are the terms *original sin* and *personal sin*. Original sin refers to the sin that Adam committed. Personal sin refers to the sins that a person commits himself.

The first half of God's salvation is negative. The Lord's death solves the problem of sin for us. He has redeemed us, purchasing us, as sinners, back. This is what the Lord's death has accomplished for us. In addition to this, He has resurrected and has come to live in us as our life. The negative redemption plus the positive saving equals salvation. His redeeming death solves all the negative, objective problems outside of us. But the problem in our inward nature can only be solved by the Lord's coming into us as life in resurrection. His life solves the five basic problems that we have. Thus, today we can reign in this life.

When we reign in life, we mainly overcome two sources. One source is sin; the other is death. In addition to these sources, there are all the negative things that belong to sin and death. None of these things are in subordination to God. Neither are they in subordination to us. Romans 8 tells us that the mind set on the flesh is enmity against God, for it is not subject to the law of God, neither indeed can it be (v. 7). Even if the mind is willing to submit, it cannot submit. This is rebellion. Sin and death are rebellion in us. All the negative things that belong to sin and death are also rebellion in us. This is the situation of man before he is saved. But now that we are saved, we can reign in this life, and everything is in subordination to us. Sin, death, and every negative thing that belongs to sin and death can do nothing with us. We have subdued them. All insubordination has to be in subjection to us. This is to reign in life to the subduing of all kinds of insubordination.

GOD JUSTIFYING THE BELIEVERS THAT THEY MAY HAVE LIFE

Romans 5:18 ends with the words "unto justification of life." This shows us that the result of justification is life. Christ has died for us, and He has redeemed us. When we believe in Christ, all the demands of God are met by Christ. He has given us Himself as our righteousness. Through this righteousness we can stand before God, and God can justify us. In addition, God gave us a gift. This gift is eternal life.

Acts 11:18 says that our repentance is unto life. Hence, both repentance and justification are for us to have God's life.

Justification Dealing with Sin for the Believers, Having Life Dealing with Death for the Believers, and the Life Received Becoming the Law of the Spirit of Life That Frees the Believers from the Law of Sin and of Death

The believers' sin is solved by justification (Rom. 5:16). But there is still "death" within the believers. Although it is called death, it is actually working very actively in man. This problem cannot be solved by justification. Life is required to solve the problem of death. Death in man causes him to be weakened to such an extent that he is dead, without any strength concerning the things of God. In this way, death reigns. But life has dealt with death for the believers (5:17). The life that the believers receive has become the law of the Spirit of life. It frees the believers from the law of sin and of death (8:2). What I can point out here is very limited. You have to dive into a deeper understanding of the matter, and you must spend time in our publications and the footnotes of the New Testament Recovery Version. In this way you will receive many riches.

GOD CAUSING THE BELIEVERS TO HAVE LIFE THAT THEY MAY REIGN IN LIFE

God has not only caused the believers to have life, but He has also caused them to reign in life. Romans 5:17a says, "For if by the offense of the one death reigned through the one...." Death reigns as a king in us. This king purposefully puts us to death. Due to the transgression of Adam, we as his descendants have a king in us who has gained control of us and who is reigning in us. Verse 17b says, "Much more those who receive the abundance of grace and of the gift of righteousness shall reign in life through the One, Jesus Christ." Justification is a gift (v. 16), and grace abounds. From this abounding grace comes a gift. This gift is righteousness. We who have inherited righteousness shall reign in life through the One, Jesus Christ. The former king was death. The latter king is those who receive grace to be justified.

But can we reign? Death is more than qualified to reign. We who are the kings do not know how to be kings. We are like the last Chinese emperor Pu-ye of the Ching Dynasty, who became emperor at the age of three. Although he was a king, he did not know how to be a king. He needed a protector to help him to be king. We who have been saved and who are justified are indeed kings, but we do not know how to be kings. Hence, through the One, Jesus Christ, who has put life in us, we are able to be kings. On the one hand, it is through this One. On the other hand, it is by reigning in life.

You have to learn to study the Bible in this way. Find out who the two kings are in Romans 5:17. The name of the first king is death. The name of the second king is your name. We are all kings today! The reason we are kings is that we are saved and have been justified. We are not only saved, but we have also received a great gift, the gift of righteousness. The grace that we have received is not a little grace, but abounding grace. It is like the abounding ocean. It is not like a cup of tea, which is gone after two sips. Grace is like an ocean. In this endless grace, God has given us a gift—abounding righteousness. Righteousness is God giving Himself to us in Christ. Furthermore, God wants us to reign. He wants to help us through the one man, Jesus Christ, with His life to reign in life.

When you go to all the villages, you should teach the people in this way. Do not try to cover too much. You will be very successful if you can teach them these ten outlines in four to six months. This will broaden their view and give them an understanding concerning salvation and the Bible. They will also be able to learn many spiritual terms. This all depends on your speaking these things clearly and accurately.

Subduing the Insubordination of Sin, Death, and All the Negative Things Belonging to Sin and Death

Every kind of addiction, such as alcohol, gambling, and theater-going, comes from sin. Moreover, every kind of addiction is rebellion. When a man is addicted to opium, he cannot live without opium. Opium smoking becomes something of rebellion. For a man to lose his temper is also something of rebellion, something related to sin. When a child refuses to obey and is naughty, we say that such a one is rebellious. According to man's fallen condition, he is rebellious in his nature. He is rebellious in his very bones and even every one of his hairs is rebellious. This rebellion brings in insubordination.

Sin Reigning unto Death, and Death Reigning through the Sinner, Causing Him to Lose All His Rights

Sin reigns unto death, and death reigns through the sinner. For example, when a couple argues, the man becomes the male king and the woman becomes the female king. Not only have they become kings in their voices, eyes, and eyelashes, even every hair on their body becomes a king. The whole family becomes a band of rebellious kings. By the end of the argument, they do not want to live anymore. This is all due to the reigning of sin and death, which cause a sinner to lose all his rights.

Grace Reigning through Righteousness unto Eternal Life, and Eternal Life through Jesus Christ Causing the Believers to Reign

We all know that grace is sweet. But grace does not have the authority. Hence, grace reigns through righteousness. God gives us grace, and He also gives us righteousness. Today we have both grace and righteousness. Grace reigns through righteousness, that is, through God Himself. The result is that man obtains eternal life. This eternal life causes the believers to reign through Jesus Christ. Romans 5:21 says, "So also grace might reign through righteousness unto eternal life through Jesus Christ our Lord." In the end, we the believers will reign in this eternal life through Jesus Christ.

Bringing in God's Kingship

When married brothers and sisters are about to clash and argue with each other, they have to declare that they are reigning through Jesus Christ. They have to declare that they will not argue anymore. This will bring in God's kingship. In a family, when the parents argue all the time, the children will become disobedient, and the whole family will be in a situation of rebellion. This family will lose the grace and right to God's blessings. What is true with a family is also true with a church. We should not consider arguments as light matters; arguments are rebellion. Arguments with proper reasons are rebellion. Arguments without proper reasons are also rebellion. What then is obedience? Obedience is to not argue and to be silent. Because I submit to the authority of the head, all my hair, tongue, lips, and teeth submit to me. They do not argue anymore, and I reign. This brings in God's kingship which expands to become the kingdom of God.

Expanding to Be the Kingdom of God, Which Is the Increase of Christ as the Seed of God's Kingdom

The kingship that is brought in as a result of our reigning in life is the expansion of Christ in us. Christ is in us as life. When your companion or your spouse is arguing, and you refrain from doing the same, you are allowing Christ to reign within, and He is expanding within you.

According to Mark 4 and Matthew 13, the kingdom of God is the Lord Jesus as the seed of life sown into the believers. This seed will develop until it becomes a sphere which is the kingdom of God. This kingdom will expand until the end of the age. At the end of the Gentile rule, we will have the condition described in Daniel 2 concerning the great image. The stone cut out without hands is the Lord Jesus (v. 34). He will come down from heaven, smite the image, and break it into pieces (v. 35). The stone will become a great mountain to fill the whole earth (2:31-35). The great mountain is the expansion of the stone.

We all hope that the Lord Jesus will come back soon. But we need to allow Him to expand His kingship in us. The more He expands in the believers, the sooner He will return. Whether He will come back sooner or not depends on whether we allow Him to expand in us. This is the kingdom of God.

CHAPTER EIGHT

LIVING THE CHURCH LIFE
IN A LOCALITY TO BE DELIVERED
FROM SELF-VIEW AND SELF-GOAL

Scripture Reading: 1 Cor. 10:32b; 12:13; Eph. 4:4a; Acts 9:31a;
Rev. 1:11; Gal. 1:2b; 2 Cor. 8:1; Rom. 16:1-5a, 16b

I. The Body of Christ being the church of God—1 Cor.
10:32b; 12:13:
 A. The Body of Christ being unique in the universe;
 the church of God also being unique in the universe—Eph. 4:4a; Acts 9:31a.
 B. The unique church of God in the universe becoming the churches in various cities locally, through
 the spread of His children over all the earth—Rev.
 1:11; Gal. 1:2b; 2 Cor. 8:1.
 C. Every believer being able to live the practical
 church life in one local church only.
II. The practical local churches in the book of Romans:
 A. The church in Cenchrea—Rom. 16:1-2:
  1. Phoebe being a deaconess there.
  2. Having been a patroness of many and of the
  apostle.
  3. Being worthy of a saint.
 B. The churches of the nations existing severally in
 various localities—16:4.
 C. The church in the house of Prisca and Aquila
 being the church in Rome—16:3, 5a.
 D. The churches of Christ being the local churches
 existing severally in various localities—16:16b.
 E. The church of which Gaius was host probably
 referring to the church in Corinth, which met in
 Gaius' house.
III. The gathering point of God's salvation in life:

A. The local churches being the gathering point of our enjoyment of God's salvation in life:
   1. Being the destination to which our enjoyment of God's salvation in life brings us.
   2. Being also the place where we continue to enjoy God's salvation in life unceasingly.
B. Saving us from self-view and self-goal.

When we live the church life in a locality, we will be saved from self-views and self-goals. Views are opinions and concepts. Goals are purposes; they come from motives. Where there is a motive, there is a goal. Only the church life can save us from our own opinions, motives, and goals.

Today, we who are in the church life should be those without any opinion. If there is to be any opinion, it should be the opinion described in Romans 12:2: "Prove by testing what the will of God is, that which is good and well-pleasing and perfect." God's perfect will is our view, opinion, and concept. Other than this, we have no concept or motive. We also have only one goal, which is to see that the Body of Christ be built up and the economy of God fulfilled. The church life is our test. It exposes all of our hearts, concepts, and motives.

THE BODY OF CHRIST BEING THE CHURCH OF GOD

The Body of Christ is unique in the universe. In the whole universe there is only one Body. The church of God is also unique in the universe. This unique church of God in the universe becomes the churches in the various cities locally in all five continents through the spread of His children over all the earth. Every believer can only live in the practical church life in one local church. If anyone is not happy with the church where he is, he may move to meet in another church. After a while, he may move to yet another place to find a church that will satisfy him. This kind of moving is not according to the will of God. God wants the believers to live the church life locally, practically, and without any opinion.

THE PRACTICAL LOCAL CHURCHES
IN THE BOOK OF ROMANS

The subject of Romans 16 is the local churches. Romans 1 talks about the just having life and living by faith (v. 17). Chapter five talks about the believers' justification unto life. Though chapter sixteen seems to only contain many verses which are just greetings, the focus of this chapter is not the greetings. This chapter shows us through the greetings the condition of the local churches at the time of Paul. The greetings manifest the condition of the churches.

First, in the church in Cenchrea, there was a sister named Phoebe who was a deaconess in the church. She had been a patroness of many and of the apostle (vv. 1-2). She was indeed worthy of being a saint. Paul hoped that the church in Rome would receive her as a noble saint and in a manner worthy of her noble status.

Second, the churches of the nations existed severally in various localities. They were not all in one locality (v. 4). Third, the church in the house of Prisca and Aquila was the church in Rome (16:3, 5a). This shows us that the number of saints in the church in Rome was probably not that large. Fourth, the churches of Christ were the local churches existing severally in various localities (16:16b). Fifth, the church of which Gaius was the host probably refers to the church in Corinth, which met in Gaius' house. All these items show us the condition of the local churches at that time.

THE GATHERING POINT OF GOD'S SALVATION IN LIFE

The local churches are the gathering point of our enjoyment of God's salvation in life. After a man is saved, he will always try to find a church. There is no saved person who does not want to find a church. This is a wonderful thing! Hence, the church is the gathering point where saints receive grace. It is the gathering point of grace. If you want to see God's grace, you have to go to the church. Hence, this is the destination of our enjoyment of God's salvation in life. The more we enjoy God's salvation in life, the more we love to go to the church meetings. This is the place where we enjoy God's salvation in life unceasingly. Finally, the result of the enjoyment of God's life is our being saved from self-view and self-goal.

CHAPTER NINE

CRUSHING SATAN UNDER OUR FEET
TO BRING IN THE KINGDOM OF GOD

Scripture Reading: Rom. 16:20; 5:17b; 14:17

I. The enjoyment of God's salvation in life causing God to soon crush Satan under our feet—Rom. 16:20:
  A. That we may enjoy the God of peace, that is, enjoy the peace of God.
  B. That we may also enjoy the grace of Christ.
II. Bringing in God's kingdom:
  A. Reigning in Christ's resurrection life—Rom. 5:17b.
  B. Expanding God's kingdom in His life—Rom. 14:17.

We must reign in life, and we must live the church life in a locality. In this way, Satan will be bound and will be crushed under our feet. The Lord said in Matthew 16 that the gates of Hades shall not overcome the built-up church (v. 18). Following this, "the kingdom of the heavens" (v. 19) is mentioned. The interchangeable use of "the kingdom of the heavens" in this verse with "the church" in the previous verse proves strongly that the genuine church is the kingdom of the heavens in this age. Hence, the church, the kingdom of God, and the dealing with Satan are all linked together. Where the church is, Satan is overcome, and the kingdom of God is brought in.

THE ENJOYMENT OF GOD'S SALVATION IN LIFE CAUSING GOD TO SOON CRUSH SATAN UNDER OUR FEET

To enjoy the God of peace is to enjoy the peace of God (Rom. 16:20). It enables us to also enjoy the grace of Christ. In the New Testament Epistles, grace and peace are always mentioned together as being with us. We must live in the church life so that Satan can be crushed under our feet and so that we can fully enjoy the Lord's grace and God's peace.

BRINGING IN GOD'S KINGDOM

Reigning in the Resurrection Life of Christ

If we live the church life in a locality, we will bring in the kingdom. The reality of this kingdom is our reigning in the resurrection life of Christ. This is not something we do by ourself, our natural being, or our own effort. This reigning and ruling is in the resurrection life of Christ.

Expanding God's Kingdom in His Life

By reigning and ruling, the sphere of God's rule will be expanded, His glory will be expressed, and His eternal purpose will be fulfilled. This is the way the kingdom of God is brought in.

Chapter Ten

THE ULTIMATE CONSUMMATION
OF GOD'S SALVATION IN LIFE—
GLORIFICATION

Scripture Reading: Rom. 8:23, 17-18, 21

I. Glorification being the transfiguration and redemption of our body—Rom. 8:23:
  A. Our body being saturated by the life of God and expressing the glory, beauty, and splendor of the life of God.
  B. Receiving sonship.
II. Glorification in the future versus the sufferings today—Rom. 8:17:
  A. The sufferings of this present time not being worthy to be compared with the coming glory to be revealed to us—Rom. 8:18.
  B. The creation also enjoying the freedom of the glory of the children of God—Rom. 8:21.
III. The Spirit as the firstfruit being the foretaste of this glorification—Rom. 8:23:
  A. The Spirit first infusing our humanity with the glory and beauty of God's life.
  B. The Spirit eventually saturating our humanity with the glory and beauty of God's life so that the divine glory and beauty in God's life is manifested as our glory.

In this message we will fellowship about the ultimate point of God's salvation in life. There is a glorious splendor to the life of God. When the Lord comes back, this life will saturate every part of our being. At that time our body will be transformed and redeemed, and we will fully enter into glory. This is the ultimate goal of God's salvation in life.

GLORIFICATION BEING THE TRANSFIGURATION
AND REDEMPTION OF OUR BODY

First, our body will be saturated by the life of God to express the glory, beauty, and splendor of the life of God. Second, we will receive the sonship. Today, we are the sons of God. But we have not fully enjoyed our sonship. Sonship denotes the blessings and enjoyment of sons. Every son inherits possessions from his father because of his sonship. The blessing of the sons of God is the coming of God Himself to be everything to His sons. The ultimate manifestation is the transfiguration, redemption, and glorification of the bodies of the sons of God. That will be the full enjoyment of the blessing of the sons of God.

GLORIFICATION IN THE FUTURE VERSUS
THE SUFFERINGS TODAY

First, the sufferings of this present time are not worthy to be compared with the coming glory to be revealed to us (Rom. 8:18). Second, the creation will also enjoy the freedom of the glory of the children of God (8:21). When we enjoy the glory in that day, all creation will also enjoy the benefit. We will enjoy freedom together. When we enter into glory with our sonship and enter into God's full manifestation, a freed atmosphere will be brought in. Today, the whole world is in an atmosphere of bondage; it is under the bondage of corruption. The only hope lies in the revelation of the sons of God. At that time the whole creation will be freed from the slavery of corruption and will enjoy the freedom of the glory of the children of God.

THE SPIRIT AS THE FIRSTFRUIT
BEING THE FORETASTE OF THIS GLORIFICATION

Today, we have the Spirit in us as the firstfruit. This is a foretaste of our enjoyment of glorification (8:23). A foretaste is like a bite in the kitchen before the meal is served. When the meal is properly served, there will be the full enjoyment. When our bodies are redeemed, that will be the time of our full enjoyment of God. Today, before that time arrives, the Spirit is in us as the foretaste. This foretaste is also a guarantee. It assures us that we will have the full enjoyment on that day. In the process, the Spirit first infuses our humanity with the glory and beauty of His life. In the end, this Spirit will saturate our humanity with the glory and beauty of His life. The divine glory and beauty of God's life will then be manifested and become our glory.

ABOUT THE AUTHOR

Witness Lee was born in 1905 in northern China and raised in a Christian family. At age 19 he was fully captured for Christ and immediately consecrated himself to preach the gospel for the rest of his life. Early in his service, he met Watchman Nee, a renowned preacher, teacher, and writer. Witness Lee labored together with Watchman Nee under his direction. In 1934 Watchman Nee entrusted Witness Lee with the responsibility for his publication operation, called the Shanghai Gospel Bookroom.

Prior to the Communist takeover in 1949, Witness Lee was sent by Watchman Nee and his other co-workers to Taiwan to ensure that the things delivered to them by the Lord would not be lost. Watchman Nee instructed Witness Lee to continue the former's publishing operation abroad as the Taiwan Gospel Bookroom, which has been publicly recognized as the publisher of Watchman Nee's works outside China. Witness Lee's work in Taiwan manifested the Lord's abundant blessing. From a mere 350 believers, newly fled from the mainland, the churches in Taiwan grew to 20,000 in five years.

In 1962 Witness Lee felt led of the Lord to come to the United States, settling in California. During his 35 years of service in the U.S., he ministered in weekly meetings and weekend conferences, delivering several thousand spoken messages. Much of his speaking has since been published as over 400 titles. Many of these have been translated into over fourteen languages. He gave his last public conference in February 1997 at the age of 91.

He leaves behind a prolific presentation of the truth in the Bible. His major work, *Life-study of the Bible,* comprises over 25,000 pages of commentary on every book of the Bible from the perspective of the believers' enjoyment and experience of God's divine life in Christ through the Holy Spirit. Witness Lee was the chief editor of a new translation of the New Testament into Chinese called the Recovery Version and directed the translation of the same into English. The Recovery Version also appears in a number of other languages. He provided an extensive body of footnotes, outlines, and spiritual cross references. A radio broadcast of his messages can be heard on Christian radio stations in the United States. In 1965 Witness Lee founded Living Stream Ministry, a non-profit corporation, located in Anaheim, California, which officially presents his and Watchman Nee's ministry.

Witness Lee's ministry emphasizes the experience of Christ as life and the practical oneness of the believers as the Body of Christ. Stressing the importance of attending to both these matters, he led the churches under his care to grow in Christian life and function. He was unbending in his conviction that God's goal is not narrow sectarianism but the Body of Christ. In time, believers began to meet simply as the church in their localities in response to this conviction. In recent years a number of new churches have been raised up in Russia and in many eastern European countries.

OTHER BOOKS PUBLISHED BY
Living Stream Ministry

Titles by Witness Lee:

Abraham—Called by God	978-0-7363-0359-0
The Experience of Life	978-0-87083-417-2
The Knowledge of Life	978-0-87083-419-6
The Tree of Life	978-0-87083-300-7
The Economy of God	978-0-87083-415-8
The Divine Economy	978-0-87083-268-0
God's New Testament Economy	978-0-87083-199-7
The World Situation and God's Move	978-0-87083-092-1
Christ vs. Religion	978-0-87083-010-5
The All-inclusive Christ	978-0-87083-020-4
Gospel Outlines	978-0-87083-039-6
Character	978-0-87083-322-9
The Secret of Experiencing Christ	978-0-87083-227-7
The Life and Way for the Practice of the Church Life	978-0-87083-785-2
The Basic Revelation in the Holy Scriptures	978-0-87083-105-8
The Crucial Revelation of Life in the Scriptures	978-0-87083-372-4
The Spirit with Our Spirit	978-0-87083-798-2
Christ as the Reality	978-0-87083-047-1
The Central Line of the Divine Revelation	978-0-87083-960-3
The Full Knowledge of the Word of God	978-0-87083-289-5
Watchman Nee—A Seer of the Divine Revelation ...	978-0-87083-625-1

Titles by Watchman Nee:

How to Study the Bible	978-0-7363-0407-8
God's Overcomers	978-0-7363-0433-7
The New Covenant	978-0-7363-0088-9
The Spiritual Man • 3 volumes	978-0-7363-0269-2
Authority and Submission	978-0-7363-0185-5
The Overcoming Life	978-1-57593-817-2
The Glorious Church	978-0-87083-745-6
The Prayer Ministry of the Church	978-0-87083-860-6
The Breaking of the Outer Man and the Release ...	978-1-57593-955-1
The Mystery of Christ	978-1-57593-954-4
The God of Abraham, Isaac, and Jacob	978-0-87083-932-0
The Song of Songs	978-0-87083-872-9
The Gospel of God • 2 volumes	978-1-57593-953-7
The Normal Christian Church Life	978-0-87083-027-3
The Character of the Lord's Worker	978-1-57593-322-1
The Normal Christian Faith	978-0-87083-748-7
Watchman Nee's Testimony	978-0-87083-051-8

Available at
Christian bookstores, or contact Living Stream Ministry
2431 W. La Palma Ave. • Anaheim, CA 92801
1-800-549-5164 • www.livingstream.com